WARHEADS

by Tarek Skylar and
Ross Berkeley Simpson

Featuring spoken word by
Suli Breaks

AF006986

written permission of the publisher. No one shall share this title, or part of this title, to any social media or file hosting websites.

The moral right of Tarek Skylar and Ross Berkeley Simpson to be identified as authors of this work has been asserted in accordance with Section 77 of the Copyright, Designs and Patents Act 1988.

USE OF COPYRIGHTED MUSIC

A licence issued by Concord Theatricals to perform this play does not include permission to use the incidental music specified in this publication. In the United Kingdom: Where the place of performance is already licensed by the PERFORMING RIGHT SOCIETY (PRS) a return of the music used must be made to them. If the place of performance is not so licensed then application should be made to PRS for Music (www.prsformusic.com). A separate and additional licence from PHONOGRAPHIC PERFORMANCE LTD (www. ppluk.com) may be needed whenever commercial recordings are used. Outside the United Kingdom: Please contact the appropriate music licensing authority in your territory for the rights to any incidental music.

USE OF COPYRIGHTED THIRD-PARTY MATERIALS

Licensees are solely responsible for obtaining formal written permission from copyright owners to use copyrighted third-party materials (e.g., artworks, logos) in the performance of this play and are strongly cautioned to do so. If no such permission is obtained by the licensee, then the licensee must use only original materials that the licensee owns and controls. Licensees are solely responsible and liable for clearances of all third-party copyrighted materials, and shall indemnify the copyright owners of the play(s) and their licensing agent, Concord Theatricals Ltd., against any costs, expenses, losses and liabilities arising from the use of such copyrighted third-party materials by licensees.

IMPORTANT BILLING AND CREDIT REQUIREMENTS

If you have obtained performance rights to this title, please refer to your licensing agreement for important billing and credit requirements.

WARHEADS was first produced by Theatre Peckham and The Bernie Grant Arts Centre in October 2018 (funded by Arts Council England). Directed by Toby Clarke, Producer Tarek (Taz) Skylar, Sound Designer Roly Botha, Lighting Designer Pablo Fernandez Baz. The cast was as follows:

MILES	Taz Skylar
DEEKS	Stevie Raine
TENA	Jahannah James
MORY	Jaz Hutchins
PHILIPA	Sarah Naudi
TEMBE	Suli Breaks

WARHEADS was produced by Park Theatre (Park90) in August 2019. Directed by Toby Clarke, Movement Director Sean Hollands, Producers Tarek (Taz) Skylar and Siobhan Walsh (As True Maverick Media) in co-production with Park Theatre, Associate Producer Markus Kartal, Sound Designer Roly Botha, Assistant Sound Designer Anja Urban, Lighting Designer Pablo Fernandez Baz. The cast was as follows:

MILES	Taz Skylar
DEEKS	Craig Fairbrass
TENA	Klariza Clayton
MORY	Hassan Najib
PHILIPA	Sophie Couch
TEMBE	Joseph Connolly

CHARACTERS

MILES WEPPLER – 22 – Caucasian and must have peroxide bleached hair.
"MORY" MORLOCK – 24 – Black.
TENA ROBINSON – 23 – Caucasian.
TEMBE – 25 – Any ethnicity but must be of the LGBTQ community.
PHILIPA KEYS – 26 – The therapist – any ethnicity.
CAPTAIN DEEKS – 40's – Any ethnicity.

AUTHOR'S NOTES

The set consists of sturdy wooden boxes, which can be moved around quickly, to form the various locations where scenes take place. The transitions between scenes are part of the story telling. How we get the boxes into place and the story we tell through movement, whilst doing it, is as important as the text itself.

ACKNOWLEDGMENTS

The journey this story has been on, all the way from conception to you reading it right now, would not have been possible without a group of angels, whose names I want to highlight:

Hassan & Gwendoline Yassin – For being the most amazing parents an unhinged boy could ever ask for.

Suli Breaks – For bending over backwards to help me get this show off the ground – asking nothing in return – and throwing yourself into a discipline which was completely unknown for you.

Ross Berkeley Simpson – For being the best writing partner I could have ever dreamt up. Your talent and the blind trust you put in me and my vision, were imperative to the journey of this piece.

Siobhan Walsh – For believing in me before anyone else did and sticking by my side when many were against.

Marz Lord – For being the guardian angel who connected our show to Park Theatre.

Jez Bond – For taking a big risk on a misfit show.

The entire team at Park Theatre – For being an absolute dream to work with.

Louise Goodman & Joe Smith at Stage One – For all their guidance, support and belief.

Robin Keynes – For being a dream mentor.

Craig Fairbrass – For choosing this to be his first play and being an inspiring figure to look up to.

Arts Council England – For giving us a chance the first time around.

Toby Clarke – For putting up with my incendiary habits and being a brilliant director.

Marcus Kartal – For being a relentless associate producer.

Jonathan Hull – For his sincere efforts to assist a cash-poor production, with any and all legal queries.

Livi Shean, Will Hollinshead & Tish Jones – For their never-ending rallying and encouragement.

Clair Dobbs – For acting as my surrogate mother, with unbelievable kindness.

Charlie Gavshon – For being my big brother, guardian, motivator and creative partner.

Alec Drysdale & Holly Marston – For being my new wonderful mentors and gracious champions going forward.

Steven Greenhalgh & Charlie Coulthard – For giving this piece a new lease of life as a published play.

I want to dedicate this play to a childhood friend of mine, who's no longer with us.

His life choices and behaviours injected this piece with life. And his spirit ignited the performances night after night.

*If I could say one last thing to you buddy, it would be this:
"I love you. And I'm going to make you proud.
We're not done down here yet. We've only just begun."*

Scene One

(A single spotlight on **WEPPLER**, *standing centre stage.* **DEEKS**, **TENA**, **TEMBE** *and* **MORLOCK** *all stand in a circle around him. Sounds of radio chatter and atmospheric music rise in volume**. *As the various sounds climax, the lights come up and* **WEPPLER** *is now lying prostrate on the ground, working on an IED – chaos happening all around him.)*

MORLOCK. Come on, bruv!

WEPPLER. What?!

MORLOCK. What you mean? Fucking what, man! Get a fucking move on.

WEPPLER. I'm busy here, bro!

MORLOCK. You know they're promised extra virgins for killing men like us!

WEPPLER. Don't use my own quote against me, Mory...

MORLOCK. Now mate, or I'm leaving...

WEPPLER. What do you mean you're fucking leaving?!

---

* A licence to produce WARHEADS does not include a performance licence for any third-party or copyrighted music. Licensees should create an original composition or use music in the public domain. For further information, please see Music Use Note on page iii.

(Lights down. Atmospheric music plays* as the scene quickly shifts. Lights up. **WEPPLER** *sits opposite* **PHILIPA**, *the young* **THERAPIST**.*)

PHILIPA. So what do you think is causing your symptoms?

WEPPLER. What's *causing* my symptoms?

PHILIPA. Yes.

WEPPLER. What symptoms?

PHILIPA. Your symptoms.

WEPPLER. My symptoms?

PHILIPA. Yes, your symptoms.

WEPPLER. I don't have any symptoms. Who told you I had symptoms?

PHILIPA. You told me you had symptoms.

WEPPLER. I told you I had symptoms?

PHILIPA. Yes, you told me you had symptoms.

WEPPLER. I'm sorry, my love, when did I tell you I had symptoms?

PHILIPA. Before. At the beginning of the session. You said you saw symptoms last night.

WEPPLER. Yeah the band... *Symptoms* is a rock band. I went to their concert last night in Camden.

PHILIPA. Miles, I just want to make sure you know... There's no judgement in this space.

WEPPLER. Okay...

---

* A licence to produce WARHEADS does not include a performance licence for any third-party or copyrighted music. Licensees should create an original composition or use music in the public domain. For further information, please see Music Use Note on page iii.

PHILIPA. I'm just saying, you're free to express anything you feel like—

(*Beat.* **WEPPLER** *considers this.*)

WEPPLER. Like discomfort?

PHILIPA. Discomfort. Okay.

And *what's* the discomfort exactly?

WEPPLER. Discomfort. You know. Discomfort, init? Like general discomfort.

PHILIPA. Difficulty sleeping?

WEPPLER. Sure.

PHILIPA. Being easily angered?

WEPPLER. You could say that.

PHILIPA. Hyperarousal.

WEPPLER. Little bit. Not gonna lie.

PHILIPA. And what do you think is causing that?

WEPPLER. See I googled it, yeah? I use Google all the time. And Google said it was the tap water that's causing my discomfort...

PHILIPA. I'm sorry... W*hat* do you think is causing it?

WEPPLER. The tap water. I know. Weird init.

(**PHILIPPA** *realising he's having her on.*)

PHILIPPA. I see. And do you think anything else might be causing it?

WEPPLER. Bruv... are you alright? I just told you it's the tap water – I mean, I've been using a new washing powder lately, but I really don't think that's it.

PHILIPA. Have you heard of PTSD?

(*Snap to* **WEPPLER***'s flat.*)

(He sits playing COD with MORY.)

WEPPLER. *(To MORLOCK.)* Bruv, is she taking the piss? Have I heard of PTSD? What, because I signed up for the front line I probably don't know ACRONYMS, is it? Cause all we did for three months, bruv, was talk about food, girls, and PTS fucking D. I know exactly what it is... so when she has the audacity to say...

(Snap back to THERAPIST's office.)

PHILIPA. Have you heard of PTSD?

(Snap back to WEPPLER's flat.)

WEPPLER. I just say...

(Snap back to THERAPIST's office.)

Nah. I don't think I have, you know. Could you explain it to me please?

PHILIPA. PTSD stands for –

WEPPLER. Penis tiny sexually disappointing.

PHILIPA. No, it stands for –

WEPPLER. Preschool therapist slurps dong.

PHILIPA. Miles –

WEPPLER. Power tennis super donkey.

PHILIPA. Post Traumatic Stress Disorder.

(Beat.)

For people like you, who have been through a lot, it's quite common. It's re-experiencing the trauma through unwanted flashbacks and nightmares. Avoidance of things that remind you of the trauma, be that people, places or things.

(WEPPLER *watches* TENA *stand up and walk towards him. He can see her, but* PHILIPA *can't.*)

Hyperarousal – as in difficulty sleeping, being easily angered... sometimes talking to oneself or to others who aren't there.

WEPPLER. *(To* TENA.*)* Well she did get that right.

PHILIPA. You're not the first patient I've talked to about this. Around eighteen per cent of veterans have some sort of PTSD.

WEPPLER. *(To* TENA.*)* In fact, she got a lot right. I should've listened. Fuck. I should have listened to a lot of people actually. Instead of just replaying things in my head. Like this.

PHILIPA. Do you think you could be experiencing any of those symptoms?

WEPPLER. *(Thinks about it.)* Nah.

(*Lights down. Music comes up. We see* WEPPLER, TENA, MORLOCK *and* TEMBE *moving the furniture for their home into the room, as a feel good song plays in the background.*[*])

Yo Tem! D'you have a boy round last night?

TENA. You didn't hear them?

WEPPLER. You should have brought him down to meet us, bro!

TEMBE. He had his hands full!

WEPPLER. He had his *what* full?

---

[*] A licence to produce WARHEADS does not include a performance licence for any third-party or copyrighted music. Licensees should create an original composition or use music in the public domain. For further information, please see Music Use Note on page iii.

TEMBE. Connect Four! We were playing Connect Four!

WEPPLER. Mory, you ready? We're going to be late!

MORY. Coming!

WEPPLER. Love, Tem. See you in a bit, T!

Scene Two

(Messy living room in a shared house. **TENA ROBINSON** *runs lines with* **TEMBE**.*)*

TENA. March to assault thy country than to tread –

Trust to't, thou shalt not – on thy mother's womb,

That brought thee to this world.

TEMBE. Yes!

TENA. Ay, and mine,

That brought you forth this boy, to keep your name

Living to time.

TEMBE. Yes!

(Then in an overly theatrical, Shakespearean voice.)

Not of a woman's tenderness to be,

Requires nor child nor woman's face to see.

I have sat too long.

TENA. Nay, go not from us thus.

If it were so that our requested did tend

To save the…

*(**TEMBE** tries to communicate the next word through charades.)*

The fuck is that?!

TEMBE. RO-MANS …

TENA. Tem! I can't do this!

TEMBE. Yes you can!

TENA. I don't even know what half these words mean!

TEMBE. Nobody knows what they mean!

TENA. Yes they do!

TEMBE. I can guarantee you Debby at the back will even laugh and she has no idea what they mean!

TENA. Fuck Shakespeare!

TEMBE. D'you want a pizza to cheer you up?

TENA. What kind of pizza?

TEMBE. What kind of pizza do you want?

TENA. What kind of pizza you getting?

TEMBE. Obviously the good kind!

TENA. From the Turkish man on Turnpike Lane?

TEMBE. Yeah.

TENA. Large pepperoni, please!

TEMBE. Do you think Wepp and Mory will want some?

TENA. They always want pizza after training night.

TEMBE. So three pepperonis, yeah?

TENA. YES!

>   (**MILES WEPPLER** *and* **"MORY" MORLOCK** *come in wearing their army uniforms. They don't look too happy.*)

WEPPLER. Hey babe!

TENA. Hey!

WEPPLER. How you doing? You okay?

TENA. I just ordered you some pizza.

WEPPLER. Aww. Bless. From Sepp's?

TENA. No from the Turkish guy on Turnpike lane.

WEPPLER. Ahh.

TENA. What? That's your favourite, right?

WEPPLER. Was my favourite, yeah. But didn't you notice – you weren't there – that when we went in there, in uniform, last week, we got a different reaction from him all of a sudden?

MORLOCK. I didn't notice that.

WEPPLER. You didn't see it? The way he looked at us was weird, man. And…

Turkish guy down the road ain't even Turkish. He's Iranian or Syrian or something like that.

MORLOCK. He's Spanish bruv.

TENA. Alright, Sepp's next time.

MORLOCK. Melissa's calling. I'll take it outside.

WEPPLER. Safe.

MORLOCK. Good luck.

WEPPLER. Safe.

*(**MORLOCK** goes outside. **TENA** goes straight for **WEPPLER**'s belt. She obviously wants to get laid. He obviously has something he needs to get off his chest first.)*

TENA. I want dick!

WEPPLER. Whoa, whoa, whoa. In the living room, T?

TENA. What? They're both upstairs…

WEPPLER. I need to tell you something first…

*(**TENA** eases off, and tries a more subtle persuasion strategy.)*

TENA. How was training?

WEPPLER. Training was good. How was your day?

TENA. Really, really good.

WEPPLER. I'm really really glad.

TENA. I'm really really glad, you're glad.

WEPPLER. How was rehearsals?

TENA. I had a day off rehearsals today, I told you that.

WEPPLER. Oh yeah, you did, sorry...

TENA. That's why I said come back as soon as you can because I wanted –

(She goes for the belt again.)

WEPPLER. Yeah – about that – just, quickly before this happens – I had a meeting with the captain today after PT –

TENA. Wait... hold on a second. I haven't seen you all day. Can you just come over here...

WEPPLER. Mm... yeah...

TENA. What's wrong?

WEPPLER. Nothing.

TENA. Do you want me to take my top off?

WEPPLER. ... Yeah...

*(**MORY** enters.)*

MORLOCK. *(Offstage.)* Yo, Wepp!

WEPPLER. What's up, bruv?

MORLOCK. *(Offstage.)* I need to talk to you.

TENA. Really? Right now?!

MORLOCK. I'm sorry, alright? Wepp.

WEPPLER. *(To **MORLOCK**.)* Bro – alright – what she say?

MORLOCK. I'm not going.

WEPPLER. What do you mean you're not going?

> *(Under his breath.)*

Shut-the-fuck-up.

MORLOCK. I can't come with you, man. I'm not doing it.

WEPPLER. What do you mean you're not doing it? Shut-the-fuck-up.

MORLOCK. I'm *not* going, man.

TENA. Going where?

WEPPLER. Babe… just give me one second, please – Shut-the-fuck-up.

TENA. Going where?

MORLOCK. Melissa just broke up with me, init.

WEPPLER. You're fucking with me!

TENA. Hello!

WEPPLER. She broke up with you?

MORLOCK. She broke up with me when I told her. Literally. Told her we was going and then boom – broken up.

TENA. Told her what?!

WEPPLER. Babe, just one second please!

TENA. NO, NOW! You need to tell me what's going on. Now.

MORLOCK. Me and Weppler are going to Afghanistan.

WEPPLER. Are you trying to fucking kill me, bro…?

> *(Beat.)*

TENA. Going where? Going where Miles? GOING WHERE?!

WEPPLER. The captain spoke to us today after training. And he offered us a slot on the next tour. And I was gonna tell you before but then you was gonna take your top off and I got real distracted. But basically me and Morlock said yeah.

(**TEMBE** *enters.*)

TEMBE. *(Add lib is needed.)* HELLOO HELLOO HELLOO, ladies. You excited for the new episode of *Stranger Things*? Heard the new episode's fucked, man. Mate, I hope they bring back Bob, he was so lovely that boy.

WEPPLER. Now's not really a good time, Tem...

TEMBE. Oh shit... what's up?

TENA. They're going on the next tour.

TEMBE. Oh shit! For real? That's mad! Like war? Like real war? Like Mad Max and that?

(**TEMBE** *realises...*)

I think I'll go watch it upstairs.

(**TEMBE** *exits upstairs.*)

WEPPLER. Tena.

TENA. You said that RESERVISTS didn't have to go.

WEPPLER. I know. I know. I know I said Reservists didn't have to go. But everything happened so quick – ask him. The captain said "We need more men out there" and then he started telling us about the salary—

TENA. Yeah but that doesn't mean you have to go.

WEPPLER. Please don't get mad. Don't get mad. Please. I wanted to tell you before. I wanted to sit you down and have a proper chat about it. Look, we got internet down there. I asked the captain. I can FaceTime you every day.

TENA. You can't FaceTime me.

WEPPLER. I can and I'll be right back. Six months isn't that long if you think about it.

TENA. SIX MONTHS?!

WEPPLER. Think about all the FaceTimes we can have!

TENA. Wow yeah can't wait!

WEPPLER. You'll wait for me right, T?

>   *(Beat.)*

TENA. Fuck you!

WEPPLER. Tena!

TENA. No. Fuck you.

WEPPLER. Fuck you!

TENA. Fuck you! You bastard!

WEPPLER. Fuck you.

TENA. Fuck-you.

WEPPLER. Okay. Fuck me then.

>   *(Beat.)*

MORLOCK. So I should just leave, yeah?

TENA. No. I think Weppler should go. For a walk.

WEPPLER. I should go for a walk?

TENA. You should go for a walk, yes.

WEPPLER. What about Mory. Shouldn't Mory go for a walk?

TENA. Mellissa's already dealt with Mory. Now I'm dealing with you. Go for a walk.

WEPPLER. But like –

TENA. Go for a walk, Miles.

WEPPLER. Aite. I'll go for a walk.

(Snap to **THERAPIST***'s office.)*

PHILIPA. Tell me about your parents.

WEPPLER. Never heard this one before… what do you wanna know about my parents?

PHILIPA. What where they like?

(Snap back to **WEPPLER***'s flat.)*

WEPPLER. *(To* **TEMBE.***)* See, Tem, she thinks I don't know what she's doing, right? That thing where she speaks really softly, almost like a paedo.

TEMBE. Ugh…

WEPPLER. Init!

See she thinks she's tuning into my subconscious with that voice.

Making me feel all relaxed and shit… when really, it just makes my dick itch.

(Back to **THERAPIST***'s office.)*

What did you wanna know about my parents again?

PHILIPA. What can you tell me about your parents?

WEPPLER. Mum was good at cooking…?

PHILIPA. And dad?

WEPPLER. Ha!

PHILIPA. Sorry, what's funny?

WEPPLER. Nothing, Dad was just a funny guy, you know…

PHILIPA. Military?

WEPPLER. Marketing, actually. He was Head of Marketing for a video game company.

PHILIPA. So you got a lot of free video games as a child?

WEPPLER. I had some, yeah.

PHILIPA. Call of Duty, Grand Theft Auto…

WEPPLER. None of your fucking business! I had that game too.

> *(Beat.)*

PHILIPA. This isn't going to work, Miles, unless you let me in.

> *(**WEPPLER** makes a fart sound with his mouth.)*

PHILIPA. Miles –

WEPPLER. What?

PHILIPA. *Miles…*

WEPPLER. *What?*

PHILIPA. If you're going to continue acting like a twelve year old…

WEPPLER. I'm sorry, ain't *you* like twelve years old?

PHILIPA. I'm twenty three.

WEPPLER. *(Fart sound.)*

PHILIPA. Are you going to let me continue?

WEPPLER. Continue, please…

PHILIPA. Alright, T –

WEPPLER. *(Fart sound.)*

PHILIPA. – Tell me about your first contact with the military. Tell me how it came about.

> *(Snaps to – open night at the Army Reserves Centre.)*

>   (**CAPTAIN DEEKS** *is stood opposite* **WEPPLER** *in his office. Pre-war.* **WEPPLER** *still has a reckless air about him, but he's much more innocent. Boyish.*)

DEEKS. Nice hair.

WEPPLER. It was a dare.

DEEKS. Funny...

WEPPLER. What the dare?

DEEKS. No, the hair.

WEPPLER. Like I said... it was a dare.

DEEKS. You think the hair makes you look like a rebel right?

WEPPLER. ...

DEEKS. Yet you don't have a cause...

WEPPLER. ...

DEEKS. A rebel without a cause is just a dickhead...

WEPPLER. Okay...

DEEKS. We can be that cause...

>   *(Beat.)*

So why do you think you have what it takes to be a part of my regiment?

WEPPLER. Because I'll keep going till I faint, sir.

DEEKS. What about all the others who say they'll keep going till they faint.

WEPPLER. They're lying, init.

>   *(Beat.)*

DEEKS. What is it you think we do exactly?

WEPPLER. I'm not sure.

DEEKS. Guess.

WEPPLER. Lift weights, shoot guns and fuck bitches?

DEEKS. Funny.

WEPPLER. Init.

DEEKS. You ever held a gun before Weppel?

WEPPLER. It's Weppler.

DEEKS. Wimpel, Pimple, Simple… I don't really care.

WEPPLER. Okidoki.

DEEKS. Have you?

WEPPLER. Have I what?

DEEKS. Held a gun before?

WEPPLER. I mean COD's pretty realistic nowadays, init.

> (**DEEKS** *walks off stage.* **WEPPLER** *is confused.* **TENA** *re-appears and crosses the stage.*)

TENA. Lift weights, shoot guns and fuck bitches? Really?

WEPPLER. Come on… I'm not really that guy, man… It's a guy thing. When guys get together, they chat shit… it's – Tena, I'm not really that guy, man. You know that.

> (*Beat.*)

Tena?

> (**DEEKS** *walks back in with a gun.*)

DEEKS. These are the toys you'll get to play with.

> (**WEPPLER** *holds it.*)

WEPPLER. Woooooo! Is it loaded?

DEEKS. Course it's not loaded…

(**WEPPLER** *aims at the audience.*)

WEPPLER. PYUME PYUME PYUME.

DEEKS. The fuck are you doing?

(*Beat.*)

WEPPLER. Making gun noises...

DEEKS. Like a baby? You're making gun noises like a baby... you know what branch of the military babies join?

(**WEPPLER** *shakes his head slowly, "no".*)

DEEKS. The infantry.

WEPPLER. Oh.

DEEKS. It's a joke. It's supposed to be funny. Babies. The Infant-ry.

WEPPLER. HAHAHAHA – I don't get it.

DEEKS. Any questions before you leave?

WEPPLER. Reservists... they're under no obligation to go to war right?

DEEKS. Not unless Britain goes into a state of emergency, no. But we ain't here to play dress up either, are we?

(*Beat.*)

I think that concludes our meeting, son.

(*Back at the* **THERAPIST**'s *office.*)

PHILIPA. But you did go to war.

WEPPLER. Fucking hell, you're smart, init?

PHILIPA. Why did you go to war?

WEPPLER. I had to do something with my life.

PHILIPA. Nothing else interested you?

WEPPLER. Tena.

PHILIPA. Tena interested you?

WEPPLER. Tena's everything to me.

PHILIPA. Then why pick a job that would make you spend so long away from her?

WEPPLER. You just don't get it, do you...? You act real smart but you're actually not – because – have you seen Tena? Have you seen me? To keep a girl like Tena, you gotta be a man. A real fucking man. You gotta have goals and shit. I didn't get good grades. Mum didn't have much money. I'm not talented. So for me, It was either work at a pizza place or join the regulars. And even though Tena says she'd love me either way... nobody ever really means that.

>   *(Snap back to flat.)*

>   *(**TENA**'s alone, in deep thought. **WEPPLER** re-enters the house.)*

Yo, T.

TENA. How was the walk?

WEPPLER. How about this?

TENA. How about what?

WEPPLER. I need to say something...

TENA. I don't think I can take anymore news.

>   *(**WEPPLER** comes down on one knee.)*

The fuck you doing?

WEPPLER. I love you so much, T.

TENA. You fucking bastard!

WEPPLER. I was kinda hoping for a yes.

TENA. Yes, you fucking bastard. I love you too. But you are kinda trapping me here. I'm pissed at you so you're gonna pull a ring out?

WEPPLER. Yeah about that, I don't actually have a ring yet –

TENA. Waw.

WEPPLER. But I love you, T!

    (**TEMBE** *enters.*)

TEMBE. *(Offstage.)* TENA is there any pizza leftover?

    (**TENA** *and* **WEPPLER** *just look at him...*)

You're proposing? That's mad, bruv! See I told you that you weren't gonna be single forever. Can I bring my mum to the wedding? Oh my God, this is gonna be so lit! Bro can you spot me for a suit?

TENA. Tem!

TEMBE. What?

TENA. Fuck off!

TEMBE. *(Then realising.)* Oh... sorry. Sorry. Sorry.

    (**TEMBE** *retreats.* **WEPPLER** *and* **TENA** *laugh.*)

TENA. Do you mean it?

WEPPLER. I mean it.

TENA. Don't say it if you don't mean it.

WEPPLER. OK. Properly. Tena Robinson. Will you marry me?

TENA. Yes! You fucking prick!

WEPPLER. Fuck off!

TENA. *(Tenderly.)* Yes...

    *(**WEPPLER** does a little dance.)*

Why? Of all times?

WEPPLER. I'm sorry – I'm sorry – I'm sorry!

    (They kiss and he spins her off as we...)

    *(Snap back to **THERAPIST**'s office.)*

PHILIPA. And Mory?

WEPPLER. What about Mory?

PHILIPA. He joined with you, correct?

WEPPLER. That is correct, yes.

PHILIPA. Were his reasons for joining the same as yours?

WEPPLER. Mory, bruv, you wanna jump in and tell baby face why you joined?

    *(To **THERAPIST**.)*

I don't know why he joined. How the fuck should I know why he joined? It looked fun on Call of Duty, init?

PHILIPA. He was your best friend.

WEPPLER. Still is my best friend.

PHILIPA. Well...

WEPPLER. Well what?

Mory! Tell her we're best friends, init.

    (Beat.)

Mory?

    *(**MORY** enters, gun in hand.)*

(We hear the noise of helicopters, bullets, tanks and explosions as we...)

(Snap to – check point in Afghanistan.)

*(**WEPPLER** and **MORLOCK** stand, holding their guns.)*

MORLOCK. And what do we do if we see anything suspicious from one of them?

WEPPLER. Point your gun and take a picture, init.

MORLOCK. That's what we're supposed to do?

WEPPLER. That's the new protocol, yeah. It changes weekly, I think.

MORLOCK. Really?

WEPPLER. Even daily, sometimes. The captain said.

MORLOCK. The captain's a cunt.

WEPPLER. Init!

*(**DEEKS** walks across the stage.)*

MORLOCK & WEPPLER. Captain!

DEEKS. At-ease.

MORLOCK. And if they shoot us whilst we're taking a photo?

WEPPLER. They won't. Probably.

MORLOCK. So point your gun, take a picture, and if they keep coming then...

WEPPLER. Then you issue them a warning, init.

MORLOCK. And then can I shoot them?

WEPPLER. Then you can shoot them. As long as you clear it with the captain first.

MORLOCK. What if the captain don't answer?

WEPPLER. You got to wait, bruv. No itchy trigger fingers in the British Army. We're not like the Americans.

MORLOCK. I gotta wait whilst an insurgent shoots at me, yeah? Cool – standard.

WEPPLER. I'm serious, bruv. If they do a report and somehow prove that you didn't clear it with the captain first, you can go to jail for that shit.

MORLOCK. I'm sure the captain won't mind me shooting back, Bruv.

WEPPLER. Captain Deeks ain't no angel, I'll give you that.

(**DEEKS** *walks across the stage.*)

MORLOCK & WEPPLER. Captain!

DEEKS. At-ease.

WEPPLER. I keep having these dreams about Tena, you know.

MORLOCK. I have dreams about your Tena too.

WEPPLER. It starts and we're just standing there and we're surrounded, yeah?

MORLOCK. Okay.

WEPPLER. And this man says – one of the men surrounding us –

MORLOCK. Mostly men, is it?

WEPPLER. He says to me. He says: "you should have stayed in Wood Green, dumbass." And shoots me, fam.

MORLOCK. What does he look like, the man?

WEPPLER. He's Black...

MORLOCK. Bit racist.

WEPPLER. I thought so too, you know.

MORLOCK. This sounds like one of your best dreams.

WEPPLER. And he hits me with a black dildo as well. It's bare weird.

MORLOCK. There are worse things you could be hit with.

WEPPLER. What do you think that means?

MORLOCK. Did you wake up with a boner?

WEPPLER. No.

MORLOCK. Then you're fine.

WEPPLER. Yeah?

MORLOCK. Yeah. It's just the twisted way your mind works.

WEPPLER. It's not that twisted. What's a boner got to do with it?

MORLOCK. Pain, bro. It's whether you enjoy pain or not.

THERAPIST. *(Voice over on the speakers.)* Well, that's not completely accurate –

>   (**MORLOCK** *suddenly points his gun at the horizon.*)

MORLOCK. What?

WEPPLER. I thought I saw something.

MORLOCK. Did you take the picture?

WEPPLER. You see it?

That figure, over there... getting closer.

MORLOCK. Should we issue a warning?

WEPPLER. Oh, I think it's just a sheep...

>   *(Beat.)*

Hey, Morlock.

MORLOCK. What?

WEPPLER. What do you call a sheep with a machine gun?

MORLOCK. Not now.

WEPPLER. A ba-a-a-a-a-a-a-d situation. Nope, not funny. Okay. I'll shut up –

That joke was Tembe's, by the way.

TEMBE. *(Voice over.)* Nah. Don't try that, bruv.

> (**WEPPLER** *looks around. Where's the voice coming from?*)

MORLOCK. What's up?

WEPPLER. I thought I heard that kid call out for me.

MORLOCK. What kid?

WEPPLER. You didn't see the kid yesterday?

MORLOCK. What kid yesterday?

WEPPLER. Ah, bruv, I didn't tell you. I was hanging out with this really cool kid yesterday, man.

MORLOCK. No luck with the ladies, then!

WEPPLER. And he goes to gimme this high five, yeah...

MORLOCK. ...and?

WEPPLER. And I didn't realise they had that shit here.

MORLOCK. What? High fives?

WEPP. Yeah and like... kids and that.

MORLOCK. You didn't think there were kids in Afghanistan? Like they was all born an adult or something?

WEPPLER. No you fucking prick. But it's like, they got kids. You get me?

MORLOCK. I really don't.

WEPPLER. Kids like our kids. Like normal kids. Doing high fives and that.

It's mad init...

MORLOCK. Yeah...

You missed a good one last night, by the way.

WEPPLER. Did I?

MORLOCK. Everyone was out.

WEPPLER. In Kabul?

MORLOCK. Yeah.

WEPPLER. I was on Skype with Tena. I miss her so much, man.

MORLOCK. My little love birds, Never forget who introduced you, will ya?

>*(Snap to a New Years Eve Party.)*
>
>*(One year ago – music*, alcohol and lots of people.* **WEPPLER** *and* **MORLOCK** *stand stage left, talking.)*

WEPPLER. I can't, man.

MORLOCK. Yes you can, man.

WEPPLER. I can't go talk to her, man.

MORLOCK. I'll introduce you.

WEPPLER. Have you seen her, bruv?

MORLOCK. Seen what?

WEPPLER. Her, man. She's way too pretty for me.

---

* A licence to produce WARHEADS does not include a performance licence for any third-party or copyrighted music. Licensees should create an original composition or use music in the public domain. For further information, please see Music Use Note on page iii.

MORLOCK. You're not that bad looking, mate.

WEPPLER. Bruv, she'll literally laugh at me if I go speak to her. She'll laugh at me.

MORLOCK. No she won't.

WEPPLER. Bruv, I look like a slim shady impersonation.

MORLOCK. She loves Eminem!

WEPPLER. I'm not doing it, man – just leave it, yeah.

MORLOCK. Alright, cool…

(Calling suddenly.)

Yo, T!!

WEPPLER. You serious right now?!

MORLOCK. Come here a second.

This is my mate I was telling you about.

TENA. Oh the one who looks like –

TENA & MORLOCK. Slim Shady…

MORLOCK. Yeah… well he was a bit too shy to come and talk to you.

TENA. So Shy Shady, yeah?

MORLOCK. So would you mind –

TENA. *(To* **WEPPLER.***)* Hey, I'm Tena!

WEPPLER. Hey… I'm Wet… I mean… I'm not wet… I'm Wepp… I'm… can I just do that again…?

TENA. Sure. Hey, I'm Tena. Also not wet…

(Beat.)

WEPPLER. Hey, I'm Miles.

TENA. Nice to meet you.

WEPPLER. Nice to meet you too.

TEMBE. Yo, T, d'you know if we got any pizza's left in the freezer?

TENA. We're all out. Mozzarella sticks in the cupboard.

TEMBE. Safe.

TENA. You wanna dance?

WEPPLER. I'm not really good at dancing so...

TENA. Really?

WEPPLER. I can two-step –

(A classic soul R&B song plays*. Triggered by **TEMBE** *and* **MORLOCK.***)*

TENA. Dance with me!

*(***WEPPLER** *does reluctantly and puts his hands on her shoulders.)*

What? Are we twelve?

(She takes his hands down to her hips.)

(They dance... until finally **WEPPLER** *trips and bangs* **TENA***'s head accidentally.)*

(Snap back to barracks in Afghanistan.)

MORLOCK. Oi, why we going back to the mosque again tomorrow?

WEPPLER. One of the American convoys got smoked by an IED yesterday so we gotta clean the area.

MORLOCK. Why are we clearing it?

---

* A licence to produce WARHEADS does not include a performance licence for any third-party or copyrighted music. Licensees should create an original composition or use music in the public domain. For further information, please see Music Use Note on page iii.

WEPPLER. Americans pussied out, init.

MORLOCK. It's bullshit, man. We've been up here four times already. Now one of the American convoys gets blown up and they want us to go clean the area? Why? What for?

WEPPLER. Well for starters, Albert's out there and he ain't complaining…

MORLOCK. We could get shot clearing the area. And even if we don't get shot and do clean the area, some Haji fucker is going to sneak back in the middle of the night and plant another ten IEDs in the same place.

WEPPLER. Bro, you work for the British Army, man, not for me.

Don't make me spend another hour convincing you, like I had to convince Albert.

If we don't clean the area a kid could get blown up? How would that sit on your conscience?

MORLOCK. Fuck them, man! Better fifty of them than one of us.

WEPPLER. Fuck off, mate. Do you hear yourself? You don't mean that.

MORLOCK. We risk our fucking lives trying to make their country safe for them and what do they do?

Do they thank us? No.

They scream at us in Pashto: "COKOLADE SARAY", "COKOLADE SARAY."

WEPPLER. *(Giggling.)* Is that what they say to you?

MORLOCK. Yeah.

WEPPLER. You sure?

MORLOCK. "COKOLADE SARAY."

They always scream that; it means: "get off my crops!"

WEPPLER. "COKOLADE SARAY", means "chocolate man," bruv.

MORLOCK. Oh. Well, racist again. But still, you get my point.

(DEEKS storms in.)

DEEKS. Contact. Contact. I repeat. We have contact. We're taking heavy fire on the east side of the village. We have casualties –

WEPPLER. Is Albert a casualty, sir?

DEEKS. Albert's dead…

WEPPLER. What?

DEEKS. Are you fucking DEAF?! Albert's dead.

WEPPLER. Mory, bruv, did you hear that, Albert's dead!

DEEKS. Get your kit together. Get your gear on. Report to the lock up in three minutes. Gear checks. Gas masks. The whole nine. We – we've got work to do. Understood?

WEPPLER & MORLOCK. Understood!

DEEKS. Understood what?

WEPPLER. Understood Captain!

(Snap back to WEPPLER's flat.)

(MORLOCK and WEPPLER sit on the sofa back at home, gaming. Call of Duty, of course.)

(TENA is with them, utterly bored.)

PYUME PYUME PYUME.

TEMBE. *(Offstage.)* Fuck off back to Afghanistan if you're gonna be making all that noise!

WEPPLER. PYUME!

MORLOCK. Bruv, can you allow the "pyume pyumes".

WEPPLER. Pyume!

MORLOCK. You're distracting me, mate.

WEPPLER. Pyume!

MORLOCK. Try doing that in Afghan, mate.

WEPPLER. Maybe I will...

(Calls.)

Yo, TEMBE!

*(**TEMBE** enters.)*

TEMBE. What?

WEPPLER. You want pizza, mate? We're ordering pizza.

TEMBE. What kind of pizza?

WEPPLER. The good kind!

TEMBE. From the Turkish guy on Turnpike Lane?

WEPPLER. No, man, that guy's shady as fuck... from the Indian guy on Green Lanes – or Sepp's.

TEMBE. Two margaritas, please.

WEPPLER. Two?

TEMBE. Yeah.

WEPPLER. You got a boy up there with you?

TEMBE. Erm... yeah.

WEPPLER. Have fun buddy!

TEMBE. Love.

TENA. Why you ordering pizzas? Let me cook you something.

WEPPLER. Nah, it's cool babe.

TENA. Uuuuh, do you want that beef dish?

WEPPLER. Nah, I'm good, honestly.

TENA. Or I could make hummus? Homemade hummus?

WEPPLER. I'm not feeling chickpeas today.

TENA. What about some Tzatziki?

WEPPLER. I really just want a pizza.

TENA. Roast chicken?

WEPPLER. Nah.

TENA. Eggs and salmon?

WEPPLER. Maybe later.

TENA. Roasted shrimp risotto with a parmesan dip?

WEPPLER. Did you just buy a new cookbook or something?

TENA. Chicken nuggets?

WEPPLER. I'm not twelve, man.

TENA. Vegan chicken nuggets?

WEPPLER. Babe!

TENA. Sorry. I'll shut up.

*(**TENA** goes to exit.)*

Do you want anything, Mory?

MORLOCK. No I – yeah, actually, could I get some of those vegan nuggets?

Please.

TENA. Sure.

MORLOCK. I think they'll go well with the pizza.

Thanks, T.

(**TENA** *exits.*)

She just wants to take care of you, man.

WEPPLER. I'm a grown ass man.

MORLOCK. And she's your grown ass girlfriend – fiancée.

WEPPLER. What's your point?

MORLOCK. Just let her be there.

WEPPLER. Bruv, don't tell me how to treat my own t'ing yeah?

MORLOCK. Safe. Do you want to switch games?

WEPPLER. I'm not playing Mario Party…

MORLOCK. *Fuck-sake –*

WEPPLER. We're staying on COD.

MORLOCK. We've been on COD for the past three hours.

WEPPLER. So?

MORLOCK. Aite… but allow the Pyumes.

WEPPLER. Safe.

MORLOCK. She cool with you going back?

WEPPLER. She's aite.

MORLOCK. Is everything alright between you two?

WEPPLER. Yeah why? What – why you asking me that? Has she said anything to you?

MORLOCK. No, course she hasn't.

(Snap back to a NYE party, on the stairs.)

*(***WEPPLER** *approaches with an ice pack.)*

WEPPLER. Sorry about bumping your head earlier…

TENA. It's fine.

WEPPLER. Like usually I'm a really good kisser, init.

TENA. Yeah, course.

WEPPLER. I never had any complaints, like…

TENA. Until now…

WEPPLER. In fact usually I get loads of compliments.

TENA. Compliments?

WEPPLER. Yeah. Bare compliments…

TENA. On your kissing?

WEPPLER. And I'm like really good at sex too.

> *(Beat.)*

TENA. Really?

WEPPLER. Yeah.

TENA. Let's go upstairs, then.

WEPPLER. What, like right now?

TENA. Talk a big game…

WEPPLER. Yeah but, like, Mory's downstairs, init. I don't wanna just leave him on his own…

TENA. He's with Melissa…

> *(Snap back to the front room.)*

WEPPLER. Oi, by the way… you heard from Melissa?

MORLOCK. Na. Nothing, bruv. Wasn't expecting to either.

WEPPLER. Ah, bruv, I should have told you earlier.

MORLOCK. Told me what?

WEPPLER. It's actually quite funny…

MORLOCK. What's funny?

WEPPLER. Yo! T! You saw Melissa earlier, init?

(**TENA** *enters.*)

TENA. Yeah, I forgot to tell you, Mory.

MORLOCK. Tell me what?

TENA. I saw her in central.

MORLOCK. And?

TENA. She's seeing someone.

MORLOCK. Hah. Who?

WEPPLER. Tell him. Tell him.

TENA. Some actor guy from Mayfair. He's in the new Christopher Nolan film or something.

WEPPLER. Hah! The war film! Playing a soldier? I told you it was funny.

Apparently he joined the Reserves to "research" for the role.

That's jokes, init.

MORLOCK. It don't feel jokes.

WEPPLER. You should be proud of that.

MORLOCK. Of what?

WEPPLER. Her t'ing is the Diet Pepsi version of you, fam. Init, Tena?

MORLOCK. You calling me fat?

WEPPLER. Shut-up, bruv. No. Her man's an actor playing a soldier. You're the real fucking deal. She couldn't have the real thing. She got the fake t'ing.

MORLOCK. Except she could.

WEPPLER. Na. Don't think like that. You could have had her if you wanted to. But you would have had to change who you are. Get some shitty office job –

MORLOCK. Or theatre job.

WEPPLER. Exactly. Playing Corio-anus or some shit like that. Fuck that.

When you say "Once more unto the breach, dear friends", you're saying it for real. You're the real fucking deal.

TENA. That's *Henry The Fifth*, you prick.

MORLOCK. Makes you wonder why she started seeing me in the first place.

WEPPLER. She's was seeing you for the same reason all the other t'ings are into us.

TENA. I'm sorry – 't'ing'?

WEPPLER. The same reason they buy hipster clothes or listen to shit jazz music on vinyl. Because they think it's cool.

(*Snap back to –* **TENA***'s old bedroom.*)

(*Same night as the house party.*)

Bruv! Are these your vinyl? I love vinyl!

TENA. Oh my god! Where'd you buy your vinyl?

WEPPLER. What?

TENA. Where'd you buy your vinyl?

WEPPLER. Harringay... vinyl shop...

TENA. Oh, I never heard of them before...

WEPPLER. Yeah, it's like a really really cool vinyl shop...

TENA. Yeah. We should go together one day...

WEPPLER. Yeah, that'd be cool...

(**TENA** *is lying on the bed – the clearest signal a guy could ever get.* **WEPPLER***'s stood at the* *other end of the room. There's an awkward silence...)*

TENA. Sorry if my room's a bit of a mess...

WEPPLER. You should see mine.

TENA. You like my new sheets?

WEPPLER. Yeah, they look bare soft. Are they cotton yeah?

TENA. Yeah. They're super soft, you should come touch them.

WEPPLER. No, I can see from here. They look bare soft.

TENA. Come touch them.

WEPPLER. Lets play some of these vinyls first – you got any jazz?! I love jazz. Jazz is the best. I love all kinds of jazz. Blues jazz, green jazz...

(Fireworks go off outside. We hear people cheer.)

TENA. Happy New Year.

WEPPLER. Happy New Year.

TENA. You planned on kissing anyone tonight?

WEPPLER. I'm not very good at planning.

*(**TENA** grabs his face and kisses him. **WEPPLER** gives in like a young boy. Then **TENA** pushes him away as he...)*

(Snaps back to front room.)

They just love to tell their friends – what is it you said in the text? "My boyfriend's in the army, he's so strong. He's so" – I'm kidding, man. Come on. It's a joke. Don't look at me like that.

Come here. You know I love you, man.

TENA. Do you wanna go for another walk?

(Snap back to **THERAPIST***'s office.)*

*(***WEPPLER** *is growing more distressed and twitchy.)*

PHILIPA. Let's talk about what followed your first tour?

WEPPLER. Mmm. No thank you.

PHILIPA. So you were already experiencing mood swings?

WEPPLER. Mmm. No.

PHILIPA. I thought you just said you were different with Tena?

WEPPLER. Mmm. Yeah.

PHILIPA. I'm sorry. I don't really understand.

WEPPLER. You could say I was different with her, yeah… but that doesn't mean I was having mood swings. That's just you trying to find some fucking reason to diagnose me.

PHILIPA. I don't *want* to diagnose you with anything. I'm just trying to find the facts.

WEPPLER. Mmm… okay.

PHILIPA. You also said earlier that you couldn't wait to get back. That you missed the… the… what was it you called them?

WEPPLER. Hajis.

PHILIPA. Hajis, yes. You missed the Hajis, you said.

MORLOCK. Bet you won't be saying you miss the Hajis after a couple of months in Kandahar?

WEPPLER. Maybe not, but at the moment, I can't wait to get out there. I actually do miss Hajis.

MORLOCK. I bet Albert don't miss the Hajis. Rest his soul.

WEPPLER. Why you got to bring up Albert again, man? Rest his soul.

(Snap to – **DEEK***'s tent in Afghanistan.)*

Collateral damage?

DEEKS. Collateral damage.

WEPPLER. Collateral damage?!

DEEKS. It happens to the best of them, soldier.

WEPPLER. With all due respect, sir, I don't think collateral damage is the official term.

DEEKS. We deal in broad strokes.

WEPPLER. Broad strokes?

DEEKS. Are you going to repeat EVERYTHING I say?

WEPPLER. Sorry if I'm a bit dumbfounded, sir. I thought we mattered.

DEEKS. I forgot how young you were, Weppler.

WEPPLER. People are scared, sir. I'm scared, sir. Half of us weren't even expecting to be out here.

DEEKS. Lift weights, shoot guns and fuck bitches. That's all we're doing out here, init?

WEPPLER. I'm glad you find this funny, sir.

DEEKS. I don't find it funny. I find it dire. But who wants to go to work when everything around them is dire?

WEPPLER. So what am I supposed to do then?!

*(***DEEKS** *turns around and invades* **WEPPLER***'s personal space.)*

DEEKS. Did I just hear you swear, soldier?

WEPPLER. No, sir.

DEEKS. Did you raise your voice?

WEPPLER. No, sir.

DEEKS. Must be the old age. Sometimes I hear things that aren't there.

WEPPLER. I mean, I always thought you looked great for your age, sir.

DEEKS. Collateral damage. That's the official term.

It's all we can do.

(Snap back to **WEPPLER***'s flat.)*

MORLOCK. Albert didn't even see it coming.

WEPPLER. What's wrong with you, man? You not looking forward to it? You're fucking lying if you say you're not.

MORLOCK. No, not really. If I had my way, I'd stay here.

WEPPLER. And do what? FUCK!

(At the game.)

Stop shooting me in the back, Mory!

MORLOCK. Stop being shit at COD.

WEPPLER. Fuck off man – and do what? What do you want to do? If you stay here.

MORLOCK. Get myself a nice little post as Staff Sergeant, training new recruits.

WEPPLER. I need you out there watching my back, Mory.

(Snap to **THERAPIST***'s office.)*

PHILIPA. Do you believe in war, Miles?

WEPPLER. I'm a soldier, init.

PHILIPA. But do you believe in war?

WEPPLER. *I'm a soldier*. Why would I be a soldier if I didn't believe in war?

PHILIPA. Many soldiers go to war without believing in it.

WEPPLER. Everyone goes to war darling. Vegans with meat eaters. Pigeons.

Ants. Even bacterias go to war.

PHILIPA. Do you think Albert believed in the war?

*(Snap back to **WEPPLER**'s flat.)*

MORLOCK. I don't want to end up like Albert!

WEPPLER. *(To **MORLOCK**.)* Look bro, Albert knew what he was getting into.

THERAPIST. How did it feel?

WEPPLER. CAN YOU STOP INTERRUPTING ME, PLEASE – IT'S INCREDIBLY ANNOYING!

*(The **THERAPIST**'s office and the flat are not clearly defined at this point. **WEPPLER** isn't sure where he is.)*

THERAPIST. Interrupting?

WEPPLER. Yeah, interrupting. It's proper rude.

THERAPIST. How did it feel to bury Albert?

WEPPLER. I didn't bury Albert.

THERAPIST. How did it feel to watch him get buried?

WEPPLER. People get buried all the time.

THERAPIST. So you could say you felt numb?

MORLOCK. I've had enough, mate. I'm going to bed.

WEPPLER. Look, bruv, you and me, we think the same way, yeah? We're bigger than this place, man. We're men!

All we fucking do here anyway is gym and Netflix. A bit of COD. Wishing we had something to do anyway.

Someone else to be with. Somewhere else to go. This isn't us mate. You know that. We're fucking warriors!

TEMBE. *(Offstage.)* Could you guys keep it down please?!

MORLOCK. Different *"warriors"* think differently.

WEPPLER. We think differently. You and me. Them? They're fucking slaves!

TEMBE. *(Offstage.)* Guys!

WEPPLER. Is that what you want, bro? To be a slave.

Seriously, I'm asking you. Is that what you want?

MORLOCK. We've had this conversation. You're not convincing me to go back on tour. I don't care what fucking Alan Watts quote you got up your sleeve. I wanna train recruits.

WEPPLER. And that's your dream, yeah? To train recruits?

MORLOCK. Maybe our dreams are just different.

WEPPLER. How different?

TENA. Hey, Mory, could you go check on the nuggets, please?

MORLOCK. Yeah, one second, Tena.

WEPPLER. Maybe you two should get a room.

MORLOCK. Shut up, mate.

TENA. You coming up, Weppy?

WEPPLER. Yeah I won't be long, T. How different?

TENA. It's just our last night, so I… ya know… got something special planned…

WEPPLER. Yeah, be right there, T – How different? Look at me and answer the fucking question.

*(**TENA** eventually leaves.)*

MORLOCK. Like, my dream isn't to get shot in the head for no man's petrol.

I got that quote from you, remember.

THERAPIST. *(To* **WEPPLER.***)* Do you believe in the war?

WEPPLER. It's not even about the war, man. He can't tell me...

THERAPIST. Who can't tell you?

WEPPLER. Fuck sake – be smarter than this – MORY. Morlock, my best friend.

HE can't tell me when a bullet from an AK grazes his face or when a mortar blows up the building next door, that shit don't make him feel alive!

MORLOCK. I just want a girl to chill with and a kid to take care of me when I'm old, man.

WEPPLER. You'll have that, bro. That's what we're fighting for as well.

When you're old and wrinkly, you're going to have a fuck-off pension as long as we make it through the next few tours.

Focus, remember your training, you'll be fine. Simples.

THERAPIST. Let's move on to your training.

(Snap to training day.)

DEEKS. Alright, lads. Today we're going to be revising efficiency of movement and how to clear a room properly under close quarters.

Understood?

WEPPLER & MORLOCK. Understood!

DEEKS. Understood what?

WEPPLER & MORLOCK. Understood, captain!

DEEKS. Now most of the time, when clearing close quarters we're gonna frag it first. But if you don't have access to your military working dog to clear the space for you, you need to have a good economy of movement. These are the things we will be evaluating today. Now, Privates Weppler and Morlock. You're up first. Assume the position.

> *(They do.)*

And – GO!

> *(**WEPPLER** and **MORLOCK** march down the aisle of the audience, turning at certain rows as if to go through doors on a hallway.)*

WEPPLER. Clear.

> *(Next door.)*

Clear.

> *(Next door.)*

Clear.

DEEKS. STOP!

WEPPLER & MORLOCK. Yes, sir.

DEEKS. First positions.

WEPPLER & MORLOCK. Yes, sir.

DEEKS. What was wrong with what you just did?

I said: what was wrong with what you just did?

WEPPLER & MORLOCK. We don't know, sir.

DEEKS. We don't know what?

WEPPLER & MORLOCK. We don't know, captain!

DEEKS. For every door, the man following must tap the shoulder of the man in front. If there is no tap. There is no move. Understood?!

WEPPLER & MORLOCK. Understood!

DEEKS. Understood what?

WNM. Understood, captain!

DEEKS. On your faces.

>   *(They assume the push-up position. For every whistle, they do a push-up.)*
>
>   *(Whistle.)*

WEPPLER & MORLOCK. One.

>   *(Whistle.)*

Two.

>   *(Whistle.)*

Three.

>   *(Whistle.)*

Four.

>   *(Whistle.)*

Five.

>   *(Whistle.)*

Six.

>   *(**TEMBE** charges in which makes us...)*
>
>   *(Snap back to **WEPPLER**'s flat.)*

TEMBE. Guys, really?!

WEPPLER. What's up, man?

TEMBE. She's not impressed, bruv. She can hear everything you're saying.

WEPPLER. We're doing some drills, brother.

MORY. YOU were...

WEPP. I told you, girls love a soldier, Tem. She's impressed. We're still waiting for you to sign up.

TEMBE. Keep waiting, bruv.

WEPPLER. Oh... still too good for it?

TEMBE. Did I say that?

MORLOCK. Leave him, man. We'll keep it down, Tem.

WEPPLER. Love, Tem. Sorry if we woke you, init.

TEMBE. Leaves.

    (**PHILIPA** *enters, which makes us...*)

    (*Snap to the* **THERAPIST**'s *office.*)

PHILIPA. And "Tem" is...?

WEPPLER. So you're just gonna keep interrupting me, yeah?

PHILIPA. You just muttered the word "TEM" –

WEPPLER. I don't "mutter", alright? Tem. Tembe. He's our housemate.

PHILIPA. And he's never been in the army?

WEPPLER. Yo, Tem! Baby face just asked if you were in the army. You wanna answer her for me, Tem?

    (*Beat.*)

Tem?

    (*Snap to* **WEPPLER**'s *flat.*)

*(We are now before **WEPPLER** moved in.)*

*(**TEMBE** is sat eating a pizza, watching Netflix in the front room with a notebook on his lap.)*

How you doing, bro? You okay?

TEMBE. Tena! Your man's here…

TENA. *(Offstage.)* I'll be down in a minute.

(Beat.)

WEPPLER. What you writing, dude?

TEMBE. POEMS.

WEPPLER. Poems? You write poems?

TEMPE. Sometimes.

WEPPLER. What kind of poem d'you write?

TEMBE. None of your business…

(Beat.)

WEPPLER. What you watching?

TEMBE. Coriolanus or something like that…

WEPPLER. The Ralph Fiennes one?

TEMBE. Yeah.

WEPPLER. Bruv, I love this film!

TEMBE. Tena! This film's shit!

TENA. *(Offstage.)* Just watch it. It gets good!

WEPPLER. So Tena's making you watch it?

TEMBE. She's in a Corio-anus play next month. She's making me watch it, so I can, like, have an idea of what's going on.

WEPPLER. What kinda films do you like?

TEMBE. Weird films...

WEPPLER. You seen Catch 22?

TEMBE. I hate Alan Arkin.

WEPPLER. Platoon?

TEMBE. What's that?

WEPPLER. What about Full Metal Jacket?

TEMBE. Ah! The one where the fat kid gets shot at the end?!

WEPPLER. Yeah – that one!

TEMBE. No, haven't see it...

WEPPLER. Oh...

> (**TEMBE** *gets up for a drink.* **WEPPLER** *looks at the notebook.* **TEMBE** *comes back.*)

TEMBE. Wanna hear my poem?

WEPPLER. Hahaha – oh shit you're serious. Sure, man. Read me your poem.

TEMBE. War

Doesn't stop the violence

It just makes it legal

It just makes it news

It just makes it so average Jo and Jane Doe can digest it with their Sunday dinner.

War.

Doesn't stop the violence

It just turns people into statistics

Victims into Martyrs.

Ideologies into weapons.

Guns and bombs into the tools required to build a nation.

And soldiers into builders.

The irony is. I once met one of these builders.

And he was broken.

Beyond repair.

WEPPLER. Nice poem, bro.

TEMBE. Listen, mate... Tena don't really go out with many guys... but, I just want you to know... if you break her heart, I'll break your toes.

WEPPLER. My toes?

TEMBE. Yes, your toes.

WEPPLER. Why you gonna break my toes, bro?

TEMBE. You asking cause you think you will?

WEPPLER. I won't.

TEMBE. Then we're fine. I won't break your toes.

Scene Three

(Sounds of people walking by. The sound of an underground station. The atmospheric music* we heard at the start is back but this time **WEPPLER**'s *line "replaying things in my head" is on repeat within the track.)*

WEPPLER. Okay, it's this one. I've been trying to think of the first moment when I knew something was really up with me, right. Like really quite fucked up. And it's none of those. It's this one. But is it, though? Fucked up, I mean. When that pizza guy looked at us like that, man, I saw something – I'm sure I did. Something extra. Something bare worrying, bruv. And he played on my mind, like – I had a few dreams about him. And in one of the dreams, he was a proper manga demon, innit. But it was just a dream, right. So why did I follow him? I literally staked out the shop like a wannabe FBI undercover twat. Had to pretend I was taking a piss when some wasteman walked down the alley. I don't know how long I was there but it was probably over an hour. In the cold. Fucking gone. And I'm even thinking it at the time – you're fucking gone, mate.

PHILIPPA. *(Voice over.)* This is a safe space...

*(***WEPPLER*** reacts to the voice. Where did it come from?)*

WEPPLER. But then he comes out the shop, waves at his little mandem who he's left to close up on his own, right. And off he zooms down the street. And all I can think is – backpack, backpack, backpack, backpack. His fucking backpack. What's in the backpack? Where's

---

* A licence to produce WARHEADS does not include a performance licence for any third-party or copyrighted music. Licensees should create an original composition or use music in the public domain. For further information, please see Music Use Note on page iii.

the backpack from? Where's he from? What's he gonna do? So I follow him, init? He's got no lazy stride, this guy is on a mission, fam. And I see he's heading toward the tube and I'm imagining seven seven, man, I'm like there, and all I can think is, should I stop him? Intercept? Knock him out so he can't blow anything up? So I just follow. And I hang back a bit in the station, by the map, cause I wanna see which route he's taking – and right before he contactlesses his way through the barrier, he does this look around – and I know. I can see what he sees. The look in his eyes. I can see what he's going to do, man. Maybe not today. But he will...

(Suddenly sounds of explosions fill the room, which makes us...)

(Snap to a battleground in Afghanistan.)

(Then, constant rifle shots fired over the voices of **MORLOCK** *and* **WEPPLER**.*)*

(They communicate with each other over radio coms.)

MORLOCK. You still love the smell of Napalm in the morning?

WEPPLER. Now is not the time!

DEEKS. *(Radio.)* Friendly forces approaching from the south. Be advised there is contact. Repeat, there is contact. Proceed with caution –

MORLOCK. No fucking shit there's contact!

DEEKS. *(Radio.)* IEDs just blew-up the east side. Civilians hurt. They got the high five kid! Repeat. They got the high five kid.

WEPPLER. What?! What?! Bruv, they got the high five kid!

MORLOCK. Fuuuuuuuuuck this!!!!

DEEKS. *(Radio.)* I repeat! They got the high five kid!

WEPPLER. You alright? Bruv, are you alright?

MORLOCK. Yeah I'm fucking marvellous.

WEPPLER. Where the fuck is air support?

MORLOCK. They said six minutes.

WEPPLER. We don't have that long. I'm too exposed.

MORLOCK. Leave the damn thing. We can make a run for it.

DEEKS. *(Radio.)* SHOTS FIRED! SHOTS FIRED!

MORLOCK. You hit?

WEPPLER. I'm bless.

MORLOCK. They're getting closer!

WEPPLER. This is fucking hard enough without people shooting at me!

MORLOCK. Wepp, you know they're promised extra virgins for killing men like you!

DEEKS. *(Radio.)* PULL BACK! PULL BACK NOW, LADS!

WEPPLER. I can't do that, captain!

MORLOCK. Why?!?!?!?!

THERAPIST. *(Voice over mixed with the sound of explosions.)* Tell me about your parents.

(A mortar blows up nearby.)

MORLOCK. What the fuck is that?

WEPPLER. RPG's.

MORLOCK. Right, that's where I draw the line mate. I don't fuck with RPGs.

WEPPLER. They're a shit shot.

MORLOCK. They've been practising.

WEPPLER. Bro, can you please for the love of Jesus Christ shut the fuck up.

I'm working on a bomb, here. You're worse than my dad in the passenger seat.

MORLOCK. You're not even qualified mate!

WEPPLER. None of us are qualified mate!

People are shooting at you. That's normal.

MORLOCK. WE HAVE TO GET OUT OF HERE NOW!

WEPPLER. I'mma cut the right wire.

MORLOCK. No!

WEPPLER. You think left, init. I can't cut the left one, bro. The left one leads outwards. Maybe to another pressure plate. I can't cut the left one, bro.

MORLOCK. WE NEED TO GO! Remember what happened to Albert!

WEPPLER. Yeah and if I don't make this trigger independent it could happen to anyone of us… we don't know where the other charges are.

MORLOCK. Now – Wepp.

WEPPLER. Morlock –

MORLOCK. Right fucking now!

WEPPLER. The fuck do you think you're doing!!!

(Massive explosions heard nearby.)

(Blackout.)

Scene Four

*(We are back in the **THERAPIST**'s office.)*

*(**WEPPLER** is holding the pliers he used to disarm the bomb in Afghan. Are they really in his hand or is it just his imagination?)*

PHILIPA. According to this report the explosion wasn't where you were standing? On the one you'd been working on?

WEPPLER. It was like five hundred metres away, connected to the same battery. But not the closest to us, no.

PHILIPA. And that's the one that killed the child? The child you'd developed a relationship with –

WEPPLER. What relationship, man? There wasn't no relationship. Make me sound like a fucking paedo or something.

PHILIPA. I just meant –

WEPPLER. He would high five me. The high five kid. If he'd see me, he'd run towards me and high five me, THAT'S IT. Even if he did have to run a bit of a way.

PHILIPA. So he'd run a long way to see you? He must have liked you. Why do you think he liked you…

WEPPLER. I like to think I'm a likeable fucking guy.

(Beat.) HA!

Alright… when I first got there I might have given him something.

I don't even remember now what it was. Might have given him some cards or boots… maybe a little bit of food and money… I don't know… something. Maybe that's why he liked me. Or maybe it wasn't.

But I – I'd see him, and high five him… that's all.

PHILIPA. Why was he outside in all that gunfire?

WEPPLER. Well I don't fucking know, do I? Maybe they'd got into his place and he was running somewhere. Maybe he was looking for me. I don't know. All I know is that the captain saw a body that could have been him, and there were no high fives anymore.

PHILIPA. And that had an effect on you?

WEPPLER. Oh fuck, man, I can't do this shit no more.

PHILIPA. I'm just trying to help –

WEPPLER. Really? You're just trying to help? Cause if you're just trying to help, you wouldn't be stood there, acting like you knew what the fuck I've been through.

PHILIPA. Well let's talk about what happened with the Turkish man.

WEPPLER. About what?

PHILIPA. About what happened with the Turkish man. The pizza guy.

(Beat.)

WEPPLER. I already told you – I just got the wrong day, okay?

PHILIPA. The wrong day?

WEPPLER. I fucking know he's planning something. I saw it, in his eyes. The look in his eyes. There was no respect for the military. He's just waiting for his moment. Him and his fucking backpack –

PHILIPA. Full of comic books –

WEPPLER. He's a fucking terrorist!

PHILIPA. He sketches pictures from comic books to pass the time on the tube and he works in a pizza place – what makes you think he's a terrorist?

WEPPLER. The look, the look! I've seen that look before.

PHILIPA. Miles, he looks at you when you're in uniform, because he sketches comic books about soldiers. He draws soldiers.

WEPPLER. How the fuck do you know what he sketches in his comic books?

PHILIPA. Why do you think he didn't press charges? You pushed him to the ground, kicked him in the head and wrestled his backpack off him.

Why do you think he didn't press charges?

WEPPLER. Because he doesn't want nothing to do with the police.

PHILIPA. Do you know that he told your girlfriend he wouldn't press charges if you received help for your condition?

WEPPLER. What condition?

PHILIPA. PTSD. Your girlfriend explained to him what you've –

WEPPLER. I told her not to go near him, man! Why is she? Listen, I don't want to do this anymore. The only reason I spoke to you is because Tena said you're confidential, you won't say anything to my friends –

PHILIPA. You have never told me your last name. That's how confidential this is.

WEPPLER. *(To* **TEMBE, DEEKS, MORLOCK** *and* **TENA.***)* BRUV! IS SHE ALRIGHT?

Does she think I don't know she could just look you up on Facebook, Tena? Does she think I'm a fucking idiot, bruv?

PHILIPA. *Who* are you talking to?

WEPPLER. What?

PHILIPA. You just turned and spoke. You've been doing it for the entire session. Sometimes you mutter words, names, sounds like… "pyumes" is it? Sometimes you speak to them directly. So… who are you talking to…?

*(**WEPPLER** looks back at them all standing on the perimeter.)*

WEPPLER. FUCK YOU, BRUV.

PHILIPA. Miles, why don't we try sitting down…?

WEPPLER. Why don't you try not fucking touching me…

PHILIPA. Miles, please…

WEPPLER. Bruv, shut the fuck up. Ain't you literally like twelve years old, fam? Who the fuck are you? All I see here are bunch of certificates on the wall that your daddy bought you, when I got scars tattooed on my fucking chest.

PHILIPA. I'm going to ask you one last time… to sit down…

WEPPLER. Fuck sitting down – fuck you!

PHILIPA. NO – FUCK YOU! FUCK YOU! SIT YOUR ARSE DOWN, WEPPLER. NOW!

WEPPLER. You know my last name?

(She composes herself.)

PHILIPA. Yes, I know your last name, Weppler. Yes, I am very sorry for swearing. I'm very sorry for raising my voice. But I am trying to help you, Miles. Yes, I'm young. Yes, my parents paid for my education. Yes. But anyone else would have had you SECTIONED by now and I didn't. Because I care. Because I believe you can be helped. I want to help you. I'm fighting for you here.

I AM FIGHTING FOR YOU. And I need you to just give me a sign.

Something. A glimmer of fucking hope that *I'm* not crazy. For thinking I can actually help you at this point.

> (**WEPPLER** *looks at the pliers in his hands. Then looks at* **PHILIPA**. *He walks to her menacingly, stops, then picks up her notebook from the floor. He goes to open it, then stops himself.*)
>
> (*He goes to hand her the notebook and as she reaches, he drops it on the ground.*)

WEPPLER. I'm done with this.

> (*Snap back to* **WEPPLER**'s *flat.*)
>
> (**TENA** *and* **MORLOCK** *stand and come into the space.*)
>
> (**WEPPLER** *sits on the sofa staring into space, twitching from his aggressive muscle spasms.* **TENA** *and* **MORLOCK** *enter laughing.*)

TENA. You all right, babe?

MORLOCK. What are you doing sitting staring at nothing, man?

Power cut or something?

WEPPLER. Where have you been?

TENA. You know where we've been.

WEPPLER. If I knew where you'd been I wouldn't be asking you, would l?

MORLOCK. We went to see her play –

WEPPLER. Shut the fuck up, I wasn't talking to you.

MORLOCK. Mate, you're fucking this up.

(**WEPPLER** *stands.*)

WEPPLER. Damn right I'm fucking this up.

TENA. Are you crazy right now?

WEPPLER. Where the fuck have you been?!

TENA. Final performance!

MORLOCK. *Coriolanus,* man.

TENA. I booked it for you, you had the – the thing – you said you didn't mind if Mory took it.

MORLOCK. But he was full of shit, apparently.

WEPPLER. Don't test me, fam.

(**TEMBE** *enters with caution.*)

TENA. I told you about it this morning. Can you actually not remember that?

WEPPLER. Tell you what I do remember, I remember you saying you had dreams about Tena. When we was on tour. The next thing I know you're coming back from a date with her.

TENA. It wasn't a date.

MORLOCK. You on drugs or something?

WEPPLER. You still testing me, fam?

MORLOCK. What's the problem?

WEPPLER. You're the problem.

MORLOCK. You've not been going to the therapist, have you?

(*Beat.*)

WEPPLER. How the fuck d'you know I've been going to a therapist?

(**WEPPLER** *charges towards* **MORLOCK**, *knocking over the furniture.* **TEMBE** *runs forward at just the right moment and gets in between them.*)

TEMBE. No, no, no – Morlock get upstairs.

MORLOCK. The therapist is there to help you, Wepp. But if you don't help yourself, there's gonna be nothing left to help.

TEMBE. Just go upstairs, Mory.

MORLOCK. Fuck this...

(**MORLOCK** *leaves.*)

WEPPLER. All right, Superman, you can go.

TEMBE. I'm not going anywhere until I know you've calmed down.

WEPPLER. Fuck off, Tem, before I make you fuck off...

TEMBE. I'm not leaving her with you when you're acting like this.

WEPPLER. Ooo is he gonna break my toes?

TEMBE. What's going on? What's going on in your head?

WEPPLER. Maybe I'm just tired, Tem. Maybe I'm just tired of living with liars and cowards.

TEMBE. Oh is that for me, yeah? A coward because I didn't sign up just because you two did.

WEPPLER. You haven't got the balls, bruv, to sign up, Tem.

TEMBE. Maybe you haven't got the balls to stay?

WEPPLER. Don't come at me with that shit, bruv. I'm the only real man in this fucking house.

TEMBE. What's a man?

Tena, he look like a man to you? He don't look like a man to me. Who was the man that helped Tena learn her lines when you was away? Who was the man with Tena on the press night for her play? Who was the man with her till three in the morning watching chick flicks cause she couldn't sleep, not knowing if you was okay?

(Beat.)

And this local terrorist pizza guy... you're fucking obsessed with...

He's from Spain. He's called Mateo. He works full time to send money back to his family in Malaga. No Isis, no Al Qaeda... He's clean! You're the one who needs sorting out. Look at what you've done. Look at how you're treating your best friend.

(Beat.)

You have a think about that. Coming, T?

TENA. I'll be fine. Thanks, though.

*(***TEMBE** *exits.)*

If you ever talk about me like that again... like I'm some next t'ing – especially when I booked those tickets for us... if you ever talk about me like that again, you won't have me anymore. You get me?

WEPPLER. I'm not the same, T.

*(**WEPPLER** is in pieces at this point. He's realised what he's done. He's obviously struggling mentally. **TENA** is shocked to see him go from so aggressive to so utterly useless.)*

TENA. I know.

WEPPLER. It's like… It's like I'm trying to wake up like… I keep finding myself… in life. You probably think this is all bare stupid, init.

TENA. No, I don't think it's bare stupid.

WEPPLER. Like, I know it sounds bare crazy, like, but it's like I'm there, but I'm not there. And then, every now and then, I really realise I'm there, in the moment. And it's like a shock. Proper shock.

Like, how the fuck did I get here kinda shock.

TENA. …

WEPPLER. I'm sorry for ditching the therapist.

(Beat.)

TENA. We can fix this.

(Snap back in Afghanistan.)

(The light implies this is a distorted memory.)

MORLOCK. Look, bro, I'm just gonna come out and say it.

I'm not gonna lie to you. I'm just gonna come out and say it. I'm not gonna lie to you. I slept with Tena. I don't even want you to get mad. I mean I – I hear you. But I needed to tell you this, because it's all starting to get a bit crazy and I've been going back and forth with this like…

*(Beat. We see **WEPPLER** struggling with this.)*

Bro it's not a thing where like – I actually love her. And I didn't mean to be in this situation like… like… I love her. And I want to marry her and like… I know you're mad, bro. I feel you. I know what you must be feeling. But I'm just being honest, I love her, init—

*(**DEEKS** enters.)*

DEEKS. On your feet!

MORLOCK. Yes, sir.

DEEKS. *(To* **WEPPLER.***)* You getting all comfortable there specialist?

MORLOCK. Yes, sir.

DEEKS. What you talking about?

MORLOCK. Nothing, sir.

DEEKS. Nothing what?

MORLOCK. Nothing, captain!

DEEKS. Your areas are looking a bit dirty lately aren't they?

   (**WEPPLER** *is in tears. Angry.*)

MORLOCK. Yes, sir!

DEEKS. Are you boys going to clean them areas or—

MORLOCK. Yes, sir!

DEEKS. YES WHAT?

MORLOCK. YES, CAPTAIN!

DEEKS. Is he alright?

MORLOCK. Yes, sir!

DEEKS. Is he crying?

MORLOCK. Yes, sir?

DEEKS. Why's he crying?

   (**WEPPLER***, now sobbing, forcefully hugs* **DEEKS***, like a young boy to his mother.*)

You better get off me, corporal.

   (**WEPPLER** *gets off him.*)

Why you crying?

WEPPLER. I don't know, sir.

DEEKS. Why's he crying?

MORLOCK. ...

DEEKS. Why's he crying, specialist? Why's he crying?

MORLOCK. I don't know, sir.

DEEKS. Why's he crying?

MORLOCK. I'm sleeping with his girlfriend.

DEEKS. What?

MORLOCK. I'm sleeping with his fiancée, sir!

DEEKS. You're sleeping with his fiancée – no wonder he's crying –

>*(To* **WEPPLER.***)*

He slept with your girl, corporal?

WEPPLER. Yes, sir.

DEEKS. *(To* **MORLOCK.***)* You're gonna wipe his tears with my shirt.

>*(***DEEKS** *takes his shirt off.)*

You're gonna wipe his tears with my shirt for sleeping with his fiancée. Now. For sleeping with his fiancée.

>*(***MORLOCK** *does.)*

And the other eye.

>*(***MORLOCK** *does.)*

Now I want you to hug him.

MORLOCK. ...

DEEKS. I want you to hug him!

MORLOCK. Yes, captain.

DEEKS. Don't make me repeat myself.

MORLOCK. Yes, captain.

    *(**MORLOCK** hugs **WEPPLER**.)*

DEEKS. Now I want you to apologise.

MORLOCK. I'm sorry.

DEEKS. For what?

MORLOCK. For sleeping with your fiancée.

DEEKS. Hug him again. Hug him properly.

MORLOCK. I'm sorry.

DEEKS. Do you accept his apology?

WEPPLER. Yes, captain.

DEEKS. Get off him. Look at me. Look at me properly. Turn around.

    *(**MORLOCK** does.)*

We're going to the mosque in ten. Gear up. Now get out of my face.

    *(**MORLOCK** sits.)*

As for you, young man. Chin up. Mosque in ten. Get ready.

    *(Snap to **WEPPLER** and **TENA**'s bedroom.)*

    *(Lights up on **TENA** and **WEPPLER** sleeping.)*

    *(**WEPPLER** suddenly jumps out of the bed, thinking he is about to attack the mosque, panting, eyes closed.)*

    *(The noise wakes **TENA** and she quickly sits up in fright.)*

TENA. Wepp – Wepp! What's the matter?! Wepp?! You're sleeping. Wepp!

    *(**WEPPLER** is panicking.)*

Look around you. Look. You're in our bedroom. You were sleeping. Calm down. There is nothing in your hands. Calm down. Relax. Relax.

    *(**WEPPLER** grabs **TENA** by the throat, eyes still closed.)*

What are you doing? What are you doing?

WEPPLER. You slept with him, didn't you?

TENA. What the fuck?

WEPPLER. I know you did – he told me!

TENA. No he fucking didn't!

WEPPLER. He did. He just told me.

TENA. What, in the dream? In the dream! You were dreaming, you fucking dickhead!

    *(**TENA** kicks him off.)*

WEPPLER. Don't treat me like a crazy person. We'll see when the chocolate baby pops out!

TENA. What baby?

    *(**WEPPLER**'s eyes open, suddenly realising what he's just done, and looks at **DEEKS**.)*

You're going back to the therapist.

WEPPLER. No I'm fucking not.

TENA. You're losing it.

WEPPLER. It was so real, T.

TENA. I'd never do that to you.

WEPPLER. It was so real though.

TENA. You can't go back on tour, you know that, right?

If you go back, I don't know what would happen to you. You need to deal with this… this, whatever it is, PTSD… I don't know… but that was definitely a night terror and that's not right.

WEPPLER. I had a nightmare, that's all, man, don't be all dramatic.

TENA. Don't do that. Don't play it off like that. You know this isn't you. You know there's something going on. You said you're not the same. You need to go and see the therapist again –

WEPPLER. Oh just fuck off, man.

TENA. Don't speak to me like that.

WEPPLER. I'm not seeing that fucking idiot again.

TENA. See someone else, then. See a doctor.

WEPPLER. As soon as I do that, that will be it. You don't get to go on a tour if they think your mind's all mashed.

TENA. You shouldn't go on a tour if your mind's all mashed. I want us to have kids, Wepp. I want to do all the things we'd already be doing if you weren't a soldier. I want that routine. I want you every night – not all this "see you in six months" bullshit.

But most of all I want you. Every time you go, a little bit less of you comes back.

If you go again…

Just go one more time…?

> *(Beat.)*

> *(**WEPPLER** shakes his head "no")*

> *(**WEPPLER** sits on the floor.)*

(TENA exits.)

(Sound and lights show us that a few hours have passed.)

(MORY enters.)

MORLOCK. You alright, mate?

WEPPLER. D'you wanna play some COD, bro?

MORLOCK. Little bit worried about you, mate.

WEPPLER. Common… I beg you let's play some COD.

MORLOCK. Listen mate, Tena told me about the nightmares you've been having…

WEPPLER. Come on, bro, let's play some COD. And I'll tell you the news.

MORLOCK. What news?

WEPPLER. My news.

MORLOCK. Which is?

WEPPLER. A secret until…

MORLOCK. Tell me the news first and then maybe we can play some COD.

WEPPLER. No matter what I say, you're still not gonna play COD, init.

MORLOCK. Try me.

WEPPLER. Tena's pregnant.

(Beat.)

MORLOCK. I think that deserves a game of COD, yeah.

WEPPLER. Oh does it?

MORLOCK. Yeah, but listen, how about we go get some fresh air first. It's almost midnight. The fireworks'll be going off in a minute.

WEPPLER. She's finally pregnant, man.

MORLOCK. Congratulations, bruv. I know you've been trying for ages, init.

So, good on ya.

WEPPLER. How did you know we'd been trying?

MORLOCK. I don't know. Look mate –

WEPPLER. She told you?

Maybe it was on date night.

MORLOCK. Check your paranoia, mate.

WEPPLER. I'm not paranoid.

MORLOCK. YES. You are!

WEPPLER. No, I'm not. We'll see when the chocolate babies pop out, won't we?

(Beat.)

MORLOCK. I say you've been trying for a long time and you talk to me like I just fucked your fiancée, mate. All I've ever cared about is you, mate. Speaking to me like this, when I joined the army for you in the first place.

WEPPLER. You didn't join the army for me, bro, you joined because you got a boner as soon as Deeks handed you an M4 on our open night.

MORLOCK. I'm twenty two, mate. I get a boner if the seat on the bus vibrates the right way. You shouldn't have read that much into it – fuck me, you're so gone – you don't even know what you've got with Tena, do you? And if someone does take it away from you, I hope you fucking know you've only got yourself to blame.

WEPPLER. You wanna say that just one more time, please?

*(We hear the fireworks. **WEPPLER** thinks they're gunshots. He yells and goes down. As if he's just been shot in the leg.)*

*(**MORLOCK** doesn't hear any war sounds. This is all happening in **WEPPLER**'s head.)*

*(**DEEKS** storms in and hands **WEPPLER** a riffle.)*

DEEKS. Weppler, they got the high five kid. They got the high five kid!

WEPPLER. What? Mory, they got the high five kid. They got the high five kid!

*(**DEEKS** runs off taking cover. Communicating over radio.)*

MORLOCK. Weppler, get up, this is not funny!

DEEKS. *(On radio.)* Weppler, hold your position!

(We hear the sound of distant gunfire.)

(On radio.) Ambush, ambush – we're surrounded this side. How many your side?

WEPPLER. At least one, captain – but I can't quite see him.

MORLOCK. *(Stunned.)* What the fuck are you doing, bro?!

DEEKS. *(On radio.)* You alive, Weppler?

WEPPLER. Alive, captain. Where's air support?

DEEKS. *(On radio.)* Not coming.

WEPPLER. Second and third squads?

DEEKS. *(On radio.)* Dead. Come round the east wall, you could pick them off from there easily – they're exposed.

Weppler, can you cover Morlock?

MORLOCK. Tembe, I need your help down here, mate!

DEEKS. *(On radio.)* Do it now, boys – they're throwing grenades.

WEPPLER. Yes, captain!

MORLOCK. TEMBE!

> *(**MORLOCK** runs off. **WEPPLER** looks around, disorientated.)*
>
> *(Massive explosion heard.)*

DEEKS. *(On radio.)* ARRRRRRRGGGHHH!

They got me, got me! Can't see my fucking legs! Can't! FUCK!

Scene Five

(**WEPPLER** *is sitting down.*)

WEPPLER. At this point I'm really struggling to figure out what's real and what's not... but the thing is, I don't even know anymore...

DEEKS. Miles.

WEPPLER. Leave me alone.

DEEKS. Miles!

WEPPLER. Leave me the fuck alone.

DEEKS. MILES!

WEPPLER. That's my name, please don't wear it the fuck out.

DEEKS. I just want to talk to you.

WEPPLER. I really don't feel like talking right now. I would appreciate it so much if everyone would just stop talking to me.

DEEKS. STAND AND FACE ME!

WEPPLER. GO FUCK YOURSELF.

DEEKS. Look, I know how hard this is, Miles. I've been there. And I know it's not pretty and I know it feels like everyone is sticking their nose in. They just want you to take the first step. All I want is for you to not slip through the cracks like I did. I'm beyond repair at this point. But there's still hope for you.

I can put you in touch with the right people. If you do it now... it might be a good idea to do it now.

    (*Beat.*)

What happened to Mory wasn't your fault mate...

(**WEPPLER** *looks* **MORLOCK** *in the eye.*)

What happened to Mory was not your fault, mate...

(**WEPPLER** *turns, gets up and turns around to* **DEEKS**. **MORLOCK** *walks towards* **WEPPLER** *and holds his shoulders.*)

What happened to Mory was not your fault, mate...

WEPPLER. *(To* **PHILIPA**.*)* This whole time, you've probably been sitting there wondering how I was gonna end up... maybe I'd fuck up the pizza guy... hurt Tena...

Fuck up myself up, even... But the thing is... we were watching the wrong guy, man...

(*A spotlight comes up on* **MORLOCK**.)

(*Snap back to* **WEPPLER**'s *flat.*)

(*Sound design: repetition of* **MORLOCK** *and* **WEPPLER**'s *lines:*)

We were watching the wrong guy...

(*The sound design of their previous lines comes to a crescendo as* **WEPPLER**'s *memory bounces back.*)

MORLOCK. *(Offstage.)* Yo, Wepp!

WEPPLER. What's up, bruv?

MORLOCK. I need to talk to you.

TENA. Really? Right now?!

MORLOCK. Melissa just broke up with me, init.

(*The spotlight lingers on* **MORLOCK** *as* **WEPPLER** *just stares at the memory of him.*)

WEPPLER. I was so caught up by my own bullshit. I couldn't even see what the fuck he was trying to tell me...

(Music and montage continues as **WEPPLER** and **MORLOCK** are now alone.)*

What's wrong with you, man? You can't speak like that. You not looking forward to it? You're fucking lying if you say you're not.

MORLOCK. No, not really. If I had my way, I'd stay here.

WEPPLER. And do what? What do you want to do, if you stay here?

MORLOCK. Get myself a nice little post as Staff Sergeant, training new recruits.

WEPPLER. I need you out there watching my back, Mory.

*(**MORLOCK** remains isolated in the light as **TENA** enters.)*

TENA. Yeah, I forgot to tell you, Mory.

MORLOCK. Tell me what?

TENA. I saw her in central.

MORLOCK. And?

TENA. She's seeing someone.

*(**WEPPLER** returns and now with each line he delivers he becomes more and more distraught – realising how much he wasn't there for him and may have even added to **MORLOCK**'s PTSD.)*

WEPPLER. Hah! The war film! Playing a soldier? I told you it was funny.

---

* A licence to produce WARHEADS does not include a performance licence for any third-party or copyrighted music. Licensees should create an original composition or use music in the public domain. For further information, please see Music Use Note on page iii.

Apparently he joined the Reserves to "research" for the role.

That's jokes, init.

MORLOCK. It don't feel jokes.

WEPPLER. We're fucking warriors!

MORLOCK. Different *"warriors"* think differently.

WEPPLER. We think differently. You and me. Them? They're fucking slaves!

Is that what you want? To be a slave?

> (**TENA** *re-enters and we snap back to* **MORLOCK** *and* **TENA** *coming back from the theatre.*)

> (**WEPPLER** *himself now becomes more and more distressed.*)

Don't test me, fam.

TENA. I told you about it this morning. Can you actually not remember that?

WEPPLER. Tell you what I do remember, I remember you saying you had dreams about Tena. When we was on tour. Then the next thing I know you're coming back from a date with her.

TENA. It wasn't a date.

MORLOCK. You on drugs or something?

WEPPLER. You still testing me, fam?

MORLOCK. What's the problem?

WEPPLER. You're the problem.

MORLOCK. You've not been going to the therapist, have you?

> (*Beat.*)

WEPPLER. How the fuck d'you know I've been going to a therapist?

> (**WEPPLER** *charges towards* **MORLOCK**. **TEMBE** *runs forward at just the right moment and gets in between them.*)

TEMBE. No, no, no – Morlock get upstairs.

MORLOCK. The therapist is there to help you, Wepp. But if you don't help yourself. There's gonna be nothing left to help.

There's gonna be nothing left to help.

There's gonna be nothing left to help.

There's gonna be nothing left to help.

There's gonna be nothing left to help.

There's gonna be nothing left to help.

> (**MORLOCK** *steps out of the centre light.*)
>
> (*The sound montage reaches a crescendo as we come back to silence and…*)
>
> (*Snap back to* **THERAPIST**'s *office.*)

WEPPLER. *(To* **PHILIPA**.*)* Mory… yeah… see I really don't want to be a pussy like… I'm sorry for saying pussy like… I really don't like being deep and that.

But, like… it's just… like… it was right in front of us the whole time, man. IT SAID "SUICIDAL" ON HIS FUCKING SHIRT FOR FUCKSAKE!

I really don't understand how we all missed it. I. I –

PHILIPA. It's okay. I understand.

WEPPLER. Really?

PHILIPA. My dad's a captain in the army… I know… you know…

WEPPLER. Thats why –

PHILIPA. Yeah...

WEPPLER. And you...

PHILIPA. Yeah...

WEPPLER. Makes sense.

PHILIPA. Sometimes.

WEPPLER. I should probably go.

PHILIPA. I'm here...

WEPPLER. If I need you right?

PHILIPA. Anytime.

WEPPLER. That would be okay?

PHILIPA. Or even if you just need –

WEPPLER. To chat or...

PHILIPA. Anything at all.

WEPPLER. Thank you.

>   *(Beat.)*

PHILIPA. Planning anything fun for the rest of the night?

WEPPLER. Yeah, Tena and Tembe and I have tickets to see a band play tonight. It's a rock band.

PHILIPA. Symptoms, by any chance?

WEPPLER. Yeah. It's in Camden.

PHILIPA. That's great.

I hope you enjoy it.

>   *(Beat.)*

Well if that's all...

WEPPLER. Pretty much.

PHILIPA. Then…

WEPPLER. I should go, init.

PHILIPA. Only if you want to…

WEPPLER. Except…

PHILIPA. What?

    (Beat.)

WEPPLER. I just…

PHILIPA. What?

    (Beat.)

Are you experiencing any…?

WEPPLER. *(Nods.)*

PHILIPA. As of late?

WEPPLER. *(Nods.)*

PHILIPA. Okay… then… let's… maybe… talk about your… symptoms?

WEPPLER. What symptoms…?

PHILIPA. Your symptoms.

WEPPLER. *(Finally acknowledging it.)* My symptoms…

    (Lights down.)

The End

ABOUT THE AUTHOR

TAREK YASSIN SKYLAR

"Taz" Tarek Yassin Skylar is a writer/actor/producer – son to a Sierra Leonese/Lebanese father and a Yorkshire mother. Raised in the Canary Islands, Tarek came to the UK four years ago after having worked at surfboard manufacturing plants, from the age of fifteen.

Dyslexic, legally illiterate, middle school dropout *(uneducated past the age of fifteen.)*, Tarek attempted to join the TA in 2016, failing his medical test after a car accident, which left him with a savage concussion. Having to wait a whole year before he could re-apply for the military, Tarek threw himself into writing and performing. *Warheads* is his first writing credit.

ABOUT THE AUTHOR

ROSS BERKELEY SIMPSON

Ross directed plays for the BAFTA-winning Television Workshop before setting up his own company, First Act Workshops, in 2009. He has written and directed many award-winning short films, including *The Present* (adapted from a script by Manda Rigby) which was described by festival judge Jonathon Coe as "an impressive achievement". In his youth Ross had a record deal with Polydor, toured with Ronan Keating and scored a No. 3 club hit in a duo with his childhood friend Louise Grice. He lives in the West Midlands.

www.ingramcontent.com/pod-product-compliance
Ingram Content Group UK Ltd.
Pitfield, Milton Keynes, MK11 3LW, UK
UKHW021840210426
5322IPUK00022B/386